Rising Above the Storm

40 days of Encouragement

By Anita Carman

Carman, Anita
Rising Above the Storm
ISBN: 978-0-9983531-1-1
Copyright ©2017 by Dreams Won't Die, LLC

Printed in the United States of America

SAN 257-1439
Published by Inspire Women
1415 S. Voss, #110-516
Houston, TX 77057

Inspire Women does not accept unsolicited manuscripts.

For additional copies of *Rising Above the Storm* or to contact
Anita Carman to speak at your event, please visit
www.inspirewomen.org or call 713-521-1609

Dedicated to Ezra Townsend Carman,
my first grandson.

INTRODUCTION

Hurricane Harvey was a rare, 1,000 year, flood event, meaning the likelihood of a flood of its scale happening, was predicted to happen only once in 1,000 years. In the span of a few days, sixty inches of rain fell in Texas. Now imagine how much rain fell when God protected Noah's family in an ark, and opened the skies to a downpour of rain on the whole earth for forty days and forty nights! More than the issue with the rain, imagine living in close quarters with family for forty days and forty nights when you've been uprooted without your usual essentials, unsure of where life is taking you, restricted to the space on an ark with hundreds of animals sharing your air space, while fenced in by family members differing in opinions and speculations for survival.

Rising Above the Storm was written on my phone in the midst of Hurricane Harvey, I jotted down thoughts while helping my son's family evacuate from a flooded house. In the midst of the upheaval and transitional living arrangements (and the arrival of a grandson shortly after the hurricane moved past Houston), the application from God's Word that I had hidden in my heart offered me practical buoyancy above the waters. I pray the publication of *Rising Above the Storm* will serve as a gift in your life, and in the lives of those you know who need encouragement to survive the storms in their lives.

Love,

Anita Carman
Founder and President
Inspire Women

Day 1

Our prayers are lifted up for all in Houston and the surrounding areas that have been impacted by the storm. I have personally survived flooding four times. I know that helpless feeling when water enters the home. I've tried negotiating with God and appealing to His mercy to spare our home. I've questioned why God allowed some events to happen. There were times, in the flurry of activity, I couldn't think at all. But in those moments when I found myself in my own thoughts, I learned to listen for and to trust in God's heartbeat rather than focus on the rhythmic pounding of the rain. I learned to not let the pattern of the rain take me on a roller coaster ride of peace and panic. I learned to get outside of my own story and to focus on the safety of those around me rather than stressing over a rug that is ruined or furniture that was afloat in my house.

Storms tested my priorities and taught me that love never fails. In the midst of the storm, it is our love for one another that will get us through. So, let us reach out and love one another! And let us pray continuously for each other!

When I pray for you I "hear" a victory song. I believe in you because I believe in the power of God's Word in you as you put His Word into action.

Love from Anita Carman

REFLECTION VERSE

[John 13:34-35] "A new command I give you: Love one another. As I have loved you, so you must love one another. By this all men will know that you are my disciples, if you love one another."

REFLECTION QUESTION

What situation is creating anxiety in your life? Instead of listening to more details that disturb you, try listening to the consistent rhythm of God's heartbeat and describe how listening for God changes you.

Day 2

Some people handle crisis better than others. Perhaps, that's because some people flex with change, while others who are more structured become overcome with stress when a force outside of their control has turned their world upside down.

In a flood, I have witnessed natural leaders rise to the occasion. Often, they are the silent ones, who may not say much during normal times but don't mince words during times of crisis. They simply do the practical things that need to be done. I have learned to value how God gave us different temperaments and how there are times for certain temperaments to rise to the occasion. The moral of the story is this: Take a back seat if you tend to panic and let the calmer personalities take the lead. We don't have to apologize for how we respond. We just need to recognize how we respond and surround ourselves with those whose temperaments are better suited to get us through a crisis. God wasn't kidding when He said He created us uniquely. So, the whole works best together. Let us appreciate each other and thank God for family and community.

When I pray for you I "hear" a victory song. I believe in you because I believe in the power of God's Word in you as you put His Word into action.

Love from Anita Carman

REFLECTION VERSE

[1 Corinthians 12:4-6] There are different kinds of gifts, but the same Spirit. There are different kinds of service, but the same Lord. There are different kinds of working, but the same God works all of them in all men.

REFLECTION QUESTION

God gives us different spiritual gifts and designed His mission to be accomplished by our combined gifts. God also gives us different temperaments by His design. How can you find blessing in the different temperaments of those around you?

Day 3

My son was expecting his first baby. My daughter-in-law had just completed the nursery. All the plans and schedules we made flew out the window in the midst of a storm. My son's house flooded. We had prayed the house would not flood. So, how do we respond to the fact that it flooded?

My daughter-in-law cried when she saw the sheetrock ripped out and the beautiful "nest" she had built broken up and scattered everywhere. For many who did not flood, we hear them say that God spared their home. But what does it mean when God allows floodwaters to enter a home? How are we to view what being blessed means?

Having survived four floods, I have learned that we are blessed whether or not floodwaters enter your home. For some, the blessing is to give to others who need help. For others, the blessing is to experience the gift of a helping hand. The overall theme that gets us through our lives, whether we're in a season of blessing or in a season of being blessed, is to experience love. There is nothing like seeing a need and reaching out to meet it, or being in a place of need and feel someone put a warm blanket around you or hand you a meal. Let us trust God's Word that love never fails and lean on love to get us through!

When I pray for you I "hear" a victory song. I believe in you because I believe in the power of God's Word in you as you put His Word into action.

Love from Anita Carman

REFLECTION VERSE

[1 Corinthians 13:8-9] Love never fails. But where there are prophecies, they will cease; where there are tongues, they will be stilled; where there is knowledge, it will pass away.

REFLECTION QUESTION

What situations are frustrating you? Instead of accusing or criticizing, how can you allow the choice to love drive your next action and the words that come out of your mouth?

Day 4

I remember the time my house flooded. I was wading through knee-deep water in my house, standing helpless, as personal items floated away. I rescued the schnauzer we had at the time because she was literally swimming and panting for her life. Meanwhile, my husband was calmly directing my two sons (if I recall correctly, they were 8 and 9 at the time) to carry what we could save to the second floor. We lived on the second floor for three months, while waiting for the house to be remodeled.

I know many who viewed our situation from the outside could not understand why we did not move. But God told us that He gave us the land and we must have the courage to possess it. He taught us that there are times He wants us to run and there are times it serves His purpose when we stay in the crisis to transform a situation. It took several years, working with those with the decision power to fix the drainage on our street, but in the end God delivered us.

Today, we don't get flooded anymore. And, after Hurricane Harvey, our home became a refuge for my son and daughter-in-law, who moved in with us after their house flooded. Interestingly, I watched my son handle a crisis and knew he had already been prepared. God does not waste our sufferings. The crisis that could have broken us became the instrument God used to make us mightier warriors. We get stronger with each opportunity to rise to the occasion.

The lesson I learned from the Bible is to watch my own responses. God was not pleased when He had parted the Red Sea for Moses and the people panicked at the next crisis. What God was waiting for was a response of faith, anchored in the history of how God had delivered us in the past and will do so again. I must admit my stomach still cramps when I stare at a new Red Sea in front of me, but every time I start to panic I tell myself, "You are not the same person this time. This time you have the foundation of having gone through it last time. Last time you were a rookie. This time you are a veteran." It helps to assess your own growth and to trust that when God grows you, He has taken you to the next level of winning battles in a fallen world.

When I pray for you I "hear" a victory song. I believe in you because I believe in the power of God's Word in you as you put His Word into action.

Love from Anita Carman

REFLECTION VERSE
[Jeremiah 12:5] If you have raced with men on foot and they have worn you out, how can you compete with horses?

REFLECTION QUESTION
Instead of focusing on the difficulties of a current situation, can you recall a time God delivered you from a similar situation? How can you draw from the strength of the past to stand as a stronger warrior?

Day 5

It's not unspiritual to grieve the loss of a home. It doesn't mean you're materialistic and have the wrong priorities. A home is more than a house. it's the hub of special moments and memories. It is the place you envisioned growing old in with your spouse or raising your children in. It's where families get together during thanksgiving and holidays. Give yourself permission to shed some tears. But then learn to refocus to join God on a different journey.

When Jesus was on earth, the Bible tells us he had no place to rest his head. He didn't have a nest because He became a refuge for those around Him. Join God on an adventure where we use our displacement to serve as a refuge for someone else. We can offer refuge in our words, in leading others to trust God, in praying for those around us. It's unsettling to be displaced out of any nest and painful when we must leave the place called home. But remember that leaving home is a temporary assignment. God designed the idea of home, and His ultimate desire is for all His children to return home. But until we arrive back at home (both our home on earth and the one in heaven) let's make the most of our assignment and love someone along the way.

When I pray for you I "hear" a victory song. I believe in you because I believe in the power of God's Word in you as you put His Word into action.

Love from Anita Carman

REFLECTION VERSE

(Matthew 8:20) Jesus replied, "Foxes have holes and birds of the air have nests, but the Son of Man has no place to lay his head."

REFLECTION QUESTION

Instead of looking for a place called home, how can you become a refuge for others around you? Instead of looking for a place of belonging, how can you reach out to those who need a place of belonging?

Day 6

Sometimes, the best way to love someone in a crisis is to let them vent; don't be too quick with the scripture verses. People need the freedom to express their losses. Then, in a moment of calm we can share how certain promises from God's Word help us through the storm.

The Bible tells us that love covers a multitude of sins. When people are under stress, they stop filtering their words and they can bruise hearts unintentionally. When people are in cramped quarters, tempers have a way of flaring. During normal times, it's easy to say, "I love you," but what happens when we are under pressure and feel life closing in on us? When someone is lashing out, perhaps the greatest act of love is to choose to overlook the outburst and remind ourselves that the situation is temporary. Offer support by simply saying, "I'm so sorry this is happening." Never make permanent decisions about a situation or about a person based on temporary events. Let us all practice to use love to cover a multitude of sins.

When I pray for you I "hear" a victory song. I believe in you because I believe in the power of God's Word in you as you put His Word into action.

Love from Anita Carman

REFLECTION VERSE

(Matthew 12:20-21) A bruised reed he will not break, and a smoldering wick he will not snuff out, till he leads justice to victory. In his name the nations will put their hope.

REFLECTION QUESTION

When people are in shock or wounded by life, they don't need our critique they need our support. How can your words and actions fan the smoldering fire in someone's heart to give them renewed hope?

_____

_____

_____

_____

_____

_____

_____

_____

_____

_____

_____

Day 7

Storms have a way of leaving a trail of destruction that requires time and effort to restore life to how it used to be. But what if God never meant for life to be restored to what it used to be? Perhaps in some cases the destruction is an opportunity to rebuild in a different way. Perhaps the next chapter of your life requires you to relocate. Perhaps you need to downsize. Or perhaps the experience was not about our physical location but more about remapping our personal relationships. Are you supposed to form a closer bond with someone you took for granted? Who are the key and important people in your life who evidenced that you were important to them as well? A storm creates, not only a crisis of relocation, but a crisis of relationship. Don't waste your crisis. Let God use crisis for your benefit.

When I pray for you I "hear" a victory song. I believe in you because I believe in the power of God's Word in you as you put His Word into action.

Love from Anita Carman

REFLECTION VERSE

[Haggai 2:9] 'The glory of this present house will be greater than the glory of the former house,' says the Lord Almighty. 'And in this place I will grant peace,' declares the Lord Almighty.

REFLECTION QUESTION

In the Old Testament the people were disappointed that the new temple they built did not appear as grand as Solomon's temple. God assessed the situation differently. He saw the new temple as more glorious because He foresaw the feet of Jesus walking in the new temple. God assesses relationship with Him as more important than our attachment to our physical belongings. How can you be less focused on restoring physical buildings and more focused on building relationship with God and with those around you?

There are times I get to experience life outside the boundaries of normal living. In responding to the flood in my son and daughter-in- law's house, I ended up storing mattress upon mattress in my house. I had to climb onto a chair to get into bed. Even Ebony, my 70-pound labradoodle, couldn't jump into bed anymore. My husband said, "You remind me of the story *The Princess and the Pea*. (Anderson, 1846) " Aha! No wonder I felt so at-home on my mattress tower! Am I not the daughter of a King?

I googled the story's title and was reminded of this well-known children's story is about a prince who created a test to see if a girl was a true princess. The secret criterion was whether she had the sensitivity to feel a single pea under layers of mattresses. She commented the next morning that she was sleepless all night because she could feel a bump in the mattress. She confirmed her royalty through her sensitivity and ended up being the prince's bride. So, in the midst of a storm, I ended up with a great story to tell my soon-to-arrive first grandson. He will tell all his friends, "My Grammy slept on a mattress that was tower-high because she's a princess and she's real sensitive to bumps in the road and loved me and my mommy and daddy through the storm!"

We create unnecessary stress for ourselves when life has to fit within our self-created boundaries. So, the mattress tower is high, so nothing is in its place, so life looks chaotic right now. It is during these times when God removes the normalcy in our lives that we find ourselves experiencing the world of boundary-less living. It doesn't have to be a scary world because, although life may look boundary-less, we are not in a free fall. Our heavenly Father hems us in and cups us in His hands. He is the boundary around our lives that is stronger than what the human eye can see. In what may feel like a free fall, God teaches us to fly.

When I pray for you I "hear" a victory song. I believe in you because I believe in the power of God's Word in you as you put His Word into action.

Love from Anita Carman

REFLECTION VERSE
[Psalm 139:5-6] You hem me in — behind and before; you have laid your hand upon me. Such knowledge is too wonderful for me, too lofty for me to attain.

REFLECTION QUESTION
What structure has God allowed to be removed from your life? How might this structure have limited your identity and kept you from stepping into God's bigger world?

_____

_____

_____

_____

_____

_____

Day 9

We don't always realize what we cling to as our anchors till they disappear from our lives. Our anchor could have been a community, a neighborhood, or a specific individual. When something like a hurricane relocates us, we may find our anchors demolished or displaced.

If you have been feeling vulnerable lately, stay close to someone who has been a consistent friend over the years. Have the humility to ask a proven friend to spend the day with you so that, in the midst of all the moving parts, you have intentionally planted something or someone unchanging in your midst. Keep your distance from unpredictable people. Their volatility will add to your angst. You will be surprised how much better you feel when you are around someone you trust. We can better handle the part of life that is changing when we begin in a place that is unchanging.

Most of all stand deeper in the Word of God. Let the reality of God's kingdom become bigger than the remnants of life that we are piecing together. Pray the "Our Father" and sink your soul in the words "thy kingdom come, thy will be done, on earth as in heaven." When God's eternal kingdom becomes present and more relevant to us than the life around us that is passing away, we won't have the same urgency for all the pieces of a world that is passing away to fit perfectly. When the dust settles, we the citizens of an eternal kingdom will still be standing.

When I pray for you, I "hear" a victory song. I believe in you because I believe in the power of God's Word in you as you put His Word into action.

Love from Anita Carman

REFLECTION VERSE

[Matthew 6:9-11] Our Father in heaven, hallowed be your name, your kingdom come, your will be done on earth as it is in heaven. Give us today our daily bread.

REFLECTION QUESTION

How do you think your current situation aligns with God's plans to bring His kingdom to earth? How can you trust God for your daily bread while joining God in what He is doing?

When you look for the blessing to unfold a specific way, you can limit God with preconceived ideas. Just because God delivered a certain way in the past, does not mean He will deliver us the same way this time. When we get into our heads that God will deliver us the same way as before we go looking for a blessing to unfold a specific way. In doing so, we box God in. We need to stop giving God the palette of colors we want Him to use. We need to just let God paint His picture. He didn't need our help when He spoke the world into existence out of nothing. He definitely did not lack vision or creativity.

So, even if you look around and everything looks like a big nothing because your world has been totally decimated, remember God began when the world was void and empty. What looks to us like a "big nothing" is God's blank canvas to paint our future. I trust in God's creativity. Let's exchange expectations of preset ideas of how God must deliver us to anchoring our hope in His artistic flare. Then, just do what we can while we are waiting to be surprised by God. Don't judge prematurely, don't accuse God, and don't box God in by telling Him what needs to happen. Let God paint outside the lines. He won't disappoint us.

When I pray for you I "hear" a victory song. I believe in you because I believe in the power of God's Word in you as you put His Word into action.

Love from Anita Carman

REFLECTION VERSE

[Genesis 1:2-3] Now the earth was a formless and empty, darkness was over the surface of the deep, and the Spirit of God was hovering over the waters. And God said, "Let there be light," and there was light.

REFLECTION QUESTION

How have you been giving God the words to say or a to-do list that aligns with your design? One word from His mouth and darkness is overtaken by light. Can you write down your to-do list you've been giving to God? Now, prayerfully tear it up and trust God to paint His picture for your life.

The challenge for responsible people is that they feel responsible. I was escaping at a hair salon when I found myself seated next to a young mom getting her hair cut. She had a stroller next to her and the baby was crying. She went on talking to the hair dresser about how she didn't like "this" and "that" about her hair cut and wanted the hair dresser to make adjustments accordingly, while the baby got louder and louder. I started feeling anxiety and was overwhelmed with the urge to pick up a stranger's baby. Then I saw a glimpse of the child and realized she was not an infant. Though still in a stroller she was old enough to walk. Her mother was not reacting because the child was having a temper tantrum. The mom was trying to teach her to wait her turn.

What I learned from that incident was not to assume others are irresponsible and need us to be responsible for them. We don't need to be saving everyone all the time. In fact, it's spiritual to disconnect as a strategy to have the energy to keep serving. Some get their nails done, some get their hair done, and some chat on the phone. Any activity that takes us out of the hustle and bustle of our usual demanding days will give our mind and body time to rest. The fact is, we replenish our soul through time with God but we replenish our body and mind through something practical that helps our body have a break. My pastor said he felt so overwhelmed with responding to needs from the hurricane that he got away by himself and bought himself a meal at a restaurant. Sometimes, we can work at being so spiritual all the time that we're no earthly good to anyone around us. It's okay to be kind to yourself. Have a coffee and dessert. Sit in the park and watch people resuming their routine of jogging. Go watch a movie that will make you laugh. God wants us to worship Him with our heart, mind, body and soul. Feel the freedom to care for all four.

When I pray for you I "hear" a victory song. I believe in you because I believe in the power of God's Word in you as you put His Word into action.

Love from Anita Carman

REFLECTION VERSE

[Mark 12:30-31] Love the Lord your God with all your heart and with all your soul and with all your mind and with all your strength. The second is this: 'Love your neighbor as yourself.' There is no commandment greater than these."

REFLECTION QUESTION

Unless we take care of the whole of us, we're not our best in serving others. What part of you have you neglected and need to honor God by taking care of your heart, mind, body, and soul?

_____

_____

_____

_____

_____

_____

_____

_____

Day 12

When I turned 18, God taught me to stop responding to the child in me. He showed me that, as an adult, I get to live life when it's unfair, when there are more needs than resources and I get to change my plans to take care of the needs around me. What keeps me from having a fit is to recognize that being grown up means having the discipline to do what's best for my family or for the ministry or for the business I'm over. The idea of doing our own thing sounds like freedom, but the end goal of life is not to do what we want to do.

Jesus did not do whatever He wanted to do. He did what the Father wanted Him to do. For Jesus, doing the Father's will meant giving up His personal preferences to do what was best for the world. Loving the way God wants us to love may mean not demanding that the insurance adjuster works only on our estimate so he can finish inspecting all the other houses in our community that flooded. Loving the way God wants us to love may mean understanding when the contractor is helping someone without a roof when we need him to bring samples for a new counter. Perhaps, the best way we can love is to wait our turn and not push our way to the front of the line. What Hurricane Harvey has done, is to redefine love to be more than sentiment or a greeting card or quoting a scripture verse to our neighbor. It's understanding that faith without works is dead and making choices of service and generosity so we, as a community, can make it together.

When I pray for you I "hear" a victory song. I believe in you because I believe in the power of God's Word in you as you put His Word into action.

Love from Anita Carman

REFLECTION VERSE

[Philippians 2:3-4] Do nothing out of selfish ambition or vain conceit, but in humility consider others better than yourselves. Each of you should look not only to your own interests, but also to the interests of others.

REFLECTION QUESTION

When you look around your neighborhood, is there someone who still needs help? When you look around your workplace or ministry, is there someone who isn't thriving and needs you to intervene? What can you do to protect not only your own welfare, but the welfare of those around you?

Day 13

Many of us who have lost our mothers find that we really miss mom during a crisis. Her absence becomes blatantly obvious when we can't just pick up the phone like we used to and vent to the person who always made time for us. She is the one who listens to our manic episodes and then offers her years of wisdom, which we discount too quickly. In our minds we're thinking, "Things have changed Mom. Your ideas won't work. Bless your heart, things are different today!" And if it's really true that Mom is out of touch with life as it is today, why do we feel compelled to call her?

I believe we call the person who offers us unconditional love because that's what we need when problems are flying at us, and we're making decisions that have major implications. We need to hear the significant woman in our life say, "Get some rest dear. You'll feel so much better tomorrow. You'll figure it out." When we feel overwhelmed and have a hard time pulling through our crisis, we need a reminder from the one who has been with us since our first breath. She is the keeper of our personal history and reminds us we've pulled through before and we'll do it again.

So, here's my salute to moms and what your encouragement means in your children's lives. For moms who have gone on to be with our Lord, we cherish the seeds of encouragement they have deposited into our spirit. We have an emotional reservoir to draw from because of what has been poured into us. And for those who never enjoyed having a mom, have the boldness to ask for one. You'll be surprised how honored someone feels when you pick them out from the crowd and say, "I need a mom relationship in my life. Will you pray about being that person to me?" At the cross, Jesus gave his mother to the disciple John to serve as John's mother. God places the lonely in families.

When I pray for you I "hear" a victory song. I believe in you because I believe in the power of God's Word in you as you put His Word into action.

Love from Anita Carman

REFLECTION VERSE

[John 19:26-27] When Jesus saw his mother there, and the disciple whom he loved standing nearby, he said to his mother, "Dear woman, here is your son," and to the disciple, "Here is your mother." From that time on, this disciple took her into his home.

REFLECTION QUESTION

When God brings two people together, the arrangement benefits both parties involved. The Apostle John needed Mary as much as Mary needed the Apostle John. Write down the relationship you long for and how you can mutually benefit the person you long for in your life. Instead of focusing on what you need, write down what you can offer. This will focus you on someone else's need instead of your own.

Day 14

There are times God feels absent. This seems especially true when our lives have been dismantled and none of the dots in our lives connect as they used to. It's hard to re-orient yourself when you've lost your anchors. You may not be in the same neighborhood anymore, you may not know where things are in a new grocery store, you're away from what used to be your anchors.

The children of Israel felt disoriented when they left their homes and were traveling with Moses to the Promise Land, a land they could only imagine and one that probably felt like a distant reality. I was thinking those displaced by Hurricane Harvey are in a similar state of transition. We have left what was once our home and are unsure when we will once again be back in a place called home. While in this state of disarray something in God's Word jumped out at me.

Did you observe the Bible tells us God spoke to His uprooted people on their way to the Promised Land from the pillar of cloud? The key word is pillar. The Bible used the word pillar with the word cloud. I don't normally think of cloud as being a pillar but more as vapor. Vapor doesn't offer me a sense of security. Vapor also feels ambivalent because the boundaries of vapor keep shifting and we're not really sure where vapor is. But the word pillar offers me the image of stone, a solid foothold, a foundation I can lean on and count on. I, for one, am grateful that God led His people as a cloud by day but described the cloud as a pillar.

So, when life feels like God is more like vapor and His will seems unclear, remind yourself that God is a pillar. He knows where He stands and He knows where He is taking us. Also, remember that while the children of Israel were led by a pillar of cloud, the Bible tells us they kept his statutes and the decrees he gave them. They were fine as long as they stuck with the plan. But when they deviated, they created their own confusion.

So here's the plan to survive the changes around you: Control your choice to keep God's Word and live by it. That's one thing we can wake up knowing will happen on a day we can't control anything else. We can control our choice to obey God's Word while trusting the pillar of cloud will lead us to our new home. Best of all, when God allows a transition, trust that His plan is to lead us to a better place than ever before.

When I pray for you I "hear" a victory song. I believe in you because I believe in the power of God's Word in you as you put His Word into action.

Love from Anita Carman

REFLECTION VERSE
[Psalm 99:7] He spoke to them from the pillar of cloud; they kept his statutes and the decrees he gave them.

REFLECTION QUESTION
When everything is changing, choose to keep something that will never change. How can you choose to obey God today as the one thing you can be sure to do in the midst of all the uncertainties in your life?

_____

_____

_____

_____

_____

Day 15

Some people adjust their perspective on a loss by escalating the loss in their minds. For example if they lost a car, they tell themselves, "At least no one was hurt!" The idea is to think of losing something even greater as a strategy to feel better about the current loss. Saying, "at least this current situation is not as bad as what it could have been," seems to work most of the time. The underlying goal to this strategy is to mitigate the pain and help us feel better. But, is avoiding pain a good coping strategy?

Although we may try to stuff our pain or run from it, I don't believe it's physically possible to detach ourselves from our losses. Our body needs a way to grieve and to process our pain. Once we become numb to our feelings, we can't feel the peaks either. Then life becomes a big blah and we lose all passion for life and the future. How do we get out of this emotional pit? One way that has worked for me is to stop talking myself out of a loss and just let myself feel the pain. Feeling pain is our way to feel life, both the good and the bad of it. When Lazarus died, Jesus wept. He did not say to himself, "Don't feel bad because you're about to raise Lazarus from the dead. So it's not that bad!" Jesus did not live disconnected from life. Though He had eternal perspective, He still allowed Himself to feel the blows of life. Losses deserve our grief if they are truly losses. From this place of authentic living, we can start to live again. Instead of saying, "Things could be worse", let us say, "I feel pain right now and everything looks bleak but this too shall pass and I expect to one day feel intensely and immensely great again! Spring and sunshine are around the corner!"

When I pray for you, I "hear" a victory song. I believe in you because I believe in the power of God's Word in you as you put His Word into action.

Love from Anita Carman

REFLECTION VERSE

[John 11:33-35] When Jesus saw her weeping, and the Jews who had come along with her also weeping, he was deeply moved in spirit and troubled. "Where have you laid him?" he asked. "Come and see, Lord," they replied. Jesus wept.

REFLECTION QUESTION

If Jesus wept when He is God and can change everything with one word, then how much more we who cannot change things with one word, should feel the freedom to weep over a loss? Write down your losses and then grieve each one of them by telling God your pain and asking Him to heal the wounds from each loss.

Day 16

A friend shared her story during the storm and gave me permission to share it with others. She spoke of the agony she felt when she saw a posting by her son of an image of himself that revealed he had been drinking. She felt helpless knowing he had an alcohol problem and was driving in the storm waters in this inebriated state. As she prayed for her son the Holy Spirit brought a scripture to her mind that surprised her. The scripture was on not coveting her neighbor. At first, she was confused over the relevance of the verse, but then she saw God had laser vision and pointed out how she resented the alcoholism in her family and had been coveting the lives of women whose children did not struggle with addiction. As soon as she accepted this verse as relevant to her life, she confessed her resentment and accepted the cross God allowed her to carry.

Hers was the cross of helping her children through their addiction to alcohol. She wanted me to know how God used the flood to purify her heart. In the midst of devastation God connects the broken parts of our lives, and makes sense of our lives. Nothing in her family's situation has changed, but there was lightness in her voice and peace in her spirit. She settled that she would accept whatever cross God chose for her to carry. Life gets redefined at the cross. On the cross on which Jesus died and on the crosses God chooses for us to carry, we nail down our personal wants and discover worship by living in God's perfect will.

When I pray for you I "hear" a victory song. I believe in you because I believe in the power of God's Word in you as you put His Word into action.

Love from Anita Carman

REFLECTION VERSE

[Mark 8:34-36] Then he called the crowd to him along with his disciples and said: "If anyone would come after me, he must deny himself and take up his cross and follow me. For whoever wants to save his life will lose it, but whoever loses his life for me and for the gospel will save it.

REFLECTION QUESTION

What cross do you resent that God has called you to carry? How can you pick up your cross and allow it to become your worship and your statement to the world that your God is worthy of your sufferings?

_____

_____

_____

_____

_____

_____

_____

_____

_____

_____

_____

_____

I found some stores fully stocked after the hurricane and discovered the job manager ordered extra supplies as soon as he heard a storm was coming. He anticipated and prepared for the needs of the people around him. What a gift we can be to others when we prepare ahead of time for their needs. I saw, fleshed out before my eyes, the value of preparation, not just for ourselves but for others.

This reminded me of how my mother used to save her pennies and hid little pockets of money around the house for those emergency times a family member or a friend might need her help. How often I have heard her say, "Here, take it!" She taught me the gift of giving. Though I found myself on the receiving end for many years after I lost her, the memory of her generosity was deposited in me.

As our city recovers, the many scenes of prevalent generosity are being deposited in us. Let us move forward into the future, seeing the evidence in our city is one of prevalent love for our neighbors of all ethnicities and economic levels, as compared to isolated incidents that point to the contrary. We have seen love and we want to continue what we have seen. Love is better. Love builds bridges. Love releases the best in all of us. Like the Bible tells us, love never fails.

When I pray for you I "hear" a victory song. I believe in you because I believe in the power of God's Word in you as you put His Word into action.

Love from Anita Carman

REFLECTION VERSE

[2 Corinthians 8:24] …show these men the proof of your love and the reason for our pride in you, so that the churches can see it.

REFLECTION QUESTION

In the New Testament times, the Apostle Paul watched for hypocrisy and showcased those who expressed genuine love. What evidence can you give God to prove your genuine love for those around you?

_____

_____

_____

_____

_____

_____

_____

_____

_____

_____

_____

_____

During Hurricane Harvey, Ebony sat at the top of the stairs watching me move around box after box of personal items from my son's flooded house. I'm not sure he understood what just happened, but I know he definitely noticed how life has changed for him. For one thing, he's always been beside me instead of being shooed out of the way. He's always been in the midst of the activity instead of being barred. Another thing I'm sure he noticed is that there were two additional canines in the house and they were sleeping on his doggy bed. But through it all, he took everything in stride because he was in tune with my emotions.

I noticed even today, he's calm when I'm calm. He takes his cue from me, his master. I have learned that I adjust better to change when I take my cue from God, my Lord and Master. He sends the sun and He sends the rain. He has His purpose for each. There are times I get to jump right into a mess and help, and there are times my role is to sit patiently and watch from afar. During the times God bars me from entering a scene my challenge is to sit still, the way Ebony sat quietly at the top of the stairs. He wasn't scratching the gate. He wasn't whining or barking. The evidence of our trust and depth of our relationship is in our ability to sit and wait. In God's perfect timing He opens the gate and we get to explore what God has been doing all the while we were waiting. Whether waiting or going, we do best when we take our cue from our Heavenly Father.

When I pray for you I "hear" a victory song. I believe in you because I believe in the power of God's Word in you as you put His Word into action.

Love from Anita Carman

REFLECTION VERSE

[John 10:25-27] Jesus answered, "… My sheep listen to my voice; I know them, and they follow me."

REFLECTION QUESTION

Whose voice is driving your frenzy? Who are you trying to please? When you press the pause button and listen for God's voice, what are His marching orders?

_____

_____

_____

_____

_____

_____

_____

_____

_____

_____

_____

_____

_____

_____

_____

The Bible says a cheerful heart is good medicine. I think when we get past the initial shock of any situation it's good to find ways to laugh. For example, my son and daughter-in-law moved in with their two dogs and a new-born baby. In addition to my pups, we now have four canines in the house. So, I said, "Let's get another dog!" Oh lol!!!

A friend of mine said, "I couldn't be bothered to put on any makeup. I don't care how I look." So I said, "Don't do it for yourself. Do it for the world and those who have to look at you!" If I had been closer she would have thrown something at me! I know it's hard to find humor when everything around us is a mess. It's hard to be positive when all you want to do is to tell everyone around you how awful everything is and how unfair life is.

But in the midst of the awfulness I think it's funny that the plants I complained about watering are now withering from being over watered. I am learning that we as humans can plan all we want but God is in control of our future. He proves that He is sovereign. What's encouraging to me is to know that God sits on His throne and everything on earth is under His authority. I trust that His thoughts towards me are for good. His plans for my life are for good. I know that when He put my family on a street that flooded He also used our family to lead the charge in solving the drainage problem and building a new road for neighbors on the whole street. I know when I lost my dream job and gave up the promotion I worked hard to get in order to follow my husband to Houston, God redirected my life and I ended up being Founder and President of Inspire Women.

I have learned that from where I sit I can't imagine the future God sees from where He sits. I've seen on plaques the saying "If mama ain't happy, ain't nobody happy!" It's true that a woman's mood sets the atmosphere in her home. The guys will roll with life, the kids get their cue from mom whether they should have fun or live in anxiety. So I have learned that the sooner I pray "Thy will be done" the sooner I have peace and put a smile back on my face and on the faces of those around me.

When I pray for you I "hear" a victory song. I believe in you because I believe in the power of God's Word in you as you put His Word into action.

Love from Anita Carman

REFLECTION VERSE

[Proverbs 19:21] Many are the plans in a man's heart, but it is the Lord's purpose that prevails.

REFLECTION QUESTION

Do you trust God's sovereignty and that He gets to decide what happens in this world? How do your responses evidence that you trust God's goodness and purpose for your life?

_____

_____

_____

_____

_____

Day 20

Well, this is definitely not one of my flattering photos, nor is it your typical image for a spiritual message! But then this thought hit me: Perhaps we need new images the world can relate to, that evidence love. So, here I am working up a sweat trying to organize all the items that arrived at my home from my son's flooded house. I was so hot and sweaty I finally changed into my bathing suit and stuck a hat on my head to get the hair out of my face. My sweet daughter-in-law is due to have the baby soon and I wanted the place to be peaceful for her. She went to work in the morning and by the time she returned home every box was unpacked or found a spot in the Carman residence. I felt the adrenaline rush of an accomplished task that paralleled that of moving a boulder!

All the while I knew that in any cleanup after a crisis there is debris on the outside that is visible, but there is also the invisible tsunami that those displaced by a storm are experiencing on the inside. What one envisioned in a place called home is abruptly changed with odds and ends that must be reassembled into a new vision. I know there are complex emotions stirring on the inside for my son and daughter-in-law, who, on their own, had just completed painting an amazing mural in the nursery. There are so many things in life I can't change for my children, but what I can do is choose how I respond. When life is out of control then regain control by controlling your choices. I choose to bring back as much order as I possibly can into the lives of my children. Whether or not my efforts made a dent, I know I did my best to love my family back to wholeness. Then I curl up on the couch, thank God for His strength and call it a great day!

When I pray for you I "hear" a victory song. I believe in you because I believe in the power of God's Word in you as you put His Word into action.

Love from Anita Carman

REFLECTION VERSE

[Ecclesiastes 11:6] Sow your seed in the morning, and at evening let not your hands be idle, for you do not know which will succeed, whether this or that, or whether both will do equally well.

REFLECTION QUESTION

What can you do to help when you're not sure what will help? There are times God will not roll out a plan but He leads us one prompting at a time. Instead of just sitting and being passive, what can you do to make things better for your family and those around you?

_____

_____

_____

_____

_____

_____

Day 21

Our expectations in life can keep us from adjusting to, and flowing with, a new plan for our lives. When we are stuck in what should be we keep ourselves from growing through what is. Over the years God continues to teach me to worship Him instead of worshipping a plan. When something unravels it's a great opportunity to ask if what we were building was what God wanted us to build or could He be redirecting us? Sometimes we should pause and not be in such a hurry to restore things to how they were. Perhaps, some things are best dismantled and rebuilt in a different way.

We free ourselves from a plan when we anchor our changes in an unchanging God. He may allow circumstances to change but His purpose is steadfast and continues from generation to generation. There are times change reveals where we have really anchored our security. Change gives us the chance to recalibrate and to put our security in a place where no event or human can unravel us. We get to determine what are essentials and what are nice to haves. I, for one, celebrate the relationships in my life. As long as I have those pillar relationships, I can cut the umbilical cord to things that can't love me back. And at the top of my most essential key relationship is an eternal God who walks with me from now till forever.

When I pray for you I "hear" a victory song. I believe in you because I believe in the power of God's Word in you as you put His Word into action.

Love from Anita Carman

REFLECTION VERSE

[James 1:17] Every good and perfect gift is from above, coming down from the Father of the heavenly lights, who does not change like shifting shadows.

REFLECTION QUESTION

Perhaps the plans you thought God had for you have changed but the truth is, God does not change. How can you anchor your life in the person of God who is changeless in His love for you as compared to anchoring your life in the plan you thought God had for you? Can you see how the change can result in something even better in your life?

Day 22

When you assess your emotions, you may find your emotional responses reaching that "over the top" level. This often happens with decisions concerning our family or home. One way I have found to open the pressure valve to my emotions, is to put on the right hat. As women we wear many hats and tend to feel responsible to take care of everyone. You may be a business leader, a ministry leader, a wife, a mother, a daughter, a granddaughter, a neighbor, etc. When I find my emotions overwhelming me I recognize that other expectations and triggers from my past may have been pressed. It could be my concept of how family relationships should work, or how home life should be. It could be many subconscious reasons I'm not even aware of, but they all feed into my anxiety level and make me insecure because life is not what it should be. Therefore, I feel like a failure.

When I find myself in this state of mind I force myself to wear the hat that helps me manage crisis, which is the hat of a business leader. As a business leader, I recognize that any time we are in a crisis we will make many decisions, some of which may need to be undone or remade. Any time decisions need to be changed, a cost of time or finances is often involved. But, when I put on my business leader hat, I make decisions knowing there will be mistakes and a cost to fix mistakes. I size up the situation at the end and not criticize myself when I miss a detail in the middle of a storm. I understand that decisions made in a crisis and in a rush situation will be imperfect. I operate with a built-in margin of error and accept an 80% rule, meaning if I can get 80% of the details right, I'm doing well.

Times of crisis showcase our imperfections. It's an opportunity to recognize how far we have fallen from perfection and need the grace of God. What a great time to pray, "Father, help me sail the ship of my family through the storm and please help everyone land safely on dry land, in spite of our mistakes."

When I pray for you I "hear" a victory song. I believe in you because I believe in the power of God's Word in you as you put His Word into action.

Love from Anita Carman

REFLECTION VERSE

[Romans 3:23-24] …for all have sinned and fall short of the glory of God, and are justified freely by his grace through the redemption that came by Christ Jesus.

REFLECTION QUESTION

How are you beating yourself up for mistakes you made in the midst of a crisis? Did you expect yourself to be flawless? How can you admit your imperfection before God and trust Him to redeem you under the power of Christ?

_____

_____

_____

_____

_____

_____

_____

Day 23

When you combine households after a flood, expect new routines to manage everyone's needs. For example, with two new pups that moved into our home, we now have four canines in the house and my family had to make practical adjustments. My husband coined a new term. He said, "We have what we call 'group pee time' and let all the dogs out at the same time." It makes life more manageable than tracking individually if each pup has gone to the bathroom. We observed that the dominant dog has wolfed down any unattended leftovers from the others and gained ten pounds. So, steps must be taken to protect her from her own lack of discipline. We noticed we might need to vacuum more often or learn not to get startled when one of the canines hears noises no one else hears and barks shrilly. None of these adjustments are earth shaking, but they can become an issue if you make it an issue.

What I have learned is that the more breathing creatures you have in the same space the more adjustments you must make. It's not a bad thing. It's simply what life is like with a big family. Ask anyone with four or more kids! There is no getting around designing routines to accommodate the needs of all breathing creatures, both human and canine. The alternative is to choose to be a hermit and shut out anyone who may have a preference that differs from yours. But the fact is, God said from the beginning that two are better than one.

Beginning in Genesis we learn that it is not good for man to be alone. The life of a hermit does not reflect the divine design. It is in community that we have the opportunity to learn how to love one another. It's so much easier to love when we are by ourselves, when I write a book about love, or when I deliver a keynote message from a stage about love. It's not possible to truly experience love when we practice the "no touch" approach. Imagine loving someone without ever getting close enough to give him or her a hug or to soothe a baby without ever holding it or rocking it. Love is not about putting up with each other, it's more about wanting to embrace change so we can be in each other's lives. It's living out the sentiment that I could not imagine you going through this storm at a time when I may no longer be on earth to call you, comfort you, or to carry you through the rough spots. It's saying, "I want it to be me! If you need a friend or family member to love you through the storm, let it be me!"

When I pray for you, I "hear" a victory song. I believe in you because I believe in the power of God's Word in you as you put His Word into action.

Love from Anita Carman

REFLECTION VERSE
[Genesis 2:18] The Lord God said, "It is not good for the man to be alone. I will make a helper suitable for him."

REFLECTION QUESTION
God designed us to live in community with each other. Whether married or single, we reflect God best when we are in community with each other. God the Father, God the Son, and God the Holy Spirit were not solo acts, but operate as one with each other. How can you better reflect the divine design by building community with those God put in your life?

_____

_____

_____

_____

_____

There are hugs and then there are hugs. Some hugs are simply an act of endearment that you display freely like saying hello or shaking someone's hands. Then there are hugs wrapping in a lifetime of friendship where we have stretched and grown together over the years. We have learned to love deeply and to forgive quickly because the longer we live, the less decades we have left to make friends that have lasted decades. We treasure our lifetime friends who have seen the good, the bad, and the ugly but love us anyway.

We cherish lifetime friends as a rare treasure, not to be discarded freely over an argument or a difference of opinion. So what if we disagree, as long as we still love each other? So what if I am not perfect or if you are not perfect, we'll be imperfectly perfect together. Sometimes it takes a flood to realize whom you would call to check on immediately, who you cannot imagine losing, and who you cannot envision being missing at the table. Then, after a flood, you learn to be kinder to each other, to show appreciation more often and thank God for friends who have doubled your joys and made the bad times bearable.

When I pray for you, I "hear" a victory song. I believe in you because I believe in the power of God's Word in you as you put His Word into action.

Love from Anita Carman

REFLECTION VERSE

[Colossians 3:13-14] Bear with each other and forgive whatever grievances you may have against one another. Forgive as the Lord forgave you. And over all these virtues put on love, which binds them all together in perfect unity.

REFLECTION QUESTION

Who have you unfriended and justified writing out of your life? What offenses are you holding onto that cannot be forgiven? As you look back over the years, how many people have you written out of your life? Do you see a pattern in them or is there a pattern in you?

Day 25

Witnessing losses around us has a way of triggering flashbacks of losses we've experienced in the past. Piling loss upon loss can be overwhelming. Instead of focusing on the loss, God has taught me to focus on His deliverance.

The fact that I am standing today is evidence that God has delivered me from a loss in the past. Meditating on our deliverance will remind us that the God who delivered us in yesteryears is the same God who has the power to deliver us today. Not only is He able, but He is willing.

He is the God who silences the raging storm outside of us and in the deepest part of our soul. He is the God who leads us to dry land. There is nothing that has happened that God has not faced before. Although this may be your first flood, this is not God's first flood. Even in the story of Noah, the end result was not total devastation but God's grace saving a family to forward His purpose. I, for one, am trusting God to continue to use believers to forward His purpose on earth. I trust God to save us to send us into our communities to represent His mercy.

When I pray for you, I hear a victory song. I believe in you because I believe in God's Word in you as you put His Word into action.

Love from Anita Carman

REFLECTION VERSE

[Psalm 86:12-13] I will praise you, O Lord my God, with all my heart; I will glorify your name forever. For great is your love toward me; you have delivered me from the depths of the grave.

REFLECTION QUESTION

Write down the times God delivered you in the past. Praise Him for each deliverance, and ask yourself if anything has changed in God's character and purpose. What would keep God from delivering you again?

_____

_____

_____

_____

_____

_____

_____

_____

_____

_____

Day 26

When our world is in disarray we stop dreaming for God, and our world gets smaller and becomes all about us. Many years ago, when I was chasing a gas leak in my house, I received a call from Beth Moore asking if I would teach her Sunday School class because she had an emergency and had to leave town. God's call through Beth hit me from left field. I justified to God why I could not possibly teach a class. Everything was in shambles at my house and I was in the middle of getting Centerpoint to check for a gas leak. It was already Thursday and the class was Sunday. I told Beth I would pray about it though I had already decided the answer was no.

Then God reminded me that it was only when King David was settled in his palace that he started to dream of building a temple for God. The lesson to me was to get things settled so I could focus on eternal things. Calling Centerpoint sufficed in settling the problem, there was no need to sit around worrying about it. Once we have done all we can do to settle the threats to our lives we can get on with the activity that forwards God's purpose. The strategy of the devil is to keep us churning so our entire focus is on staying unsettled and setting aside eternal things.

I get intentional about how I spend my time when I imagine life as grains of sand in an hour glass where the sand keeps falling as the clock to the time God has given me is running out. Every day on earth is one less day we have to live for God. The most important asset we have is our time. The faster we have taken steps to settle details that are unsettled, the sooner we get back to refocusing on what has eternal implications. So, as I watch the grains of sand in the hour glass symbolize the seconds, minutes and hours of the day that I will never get back, I choose to settle the chaos in my life so I won't miss God's purpose for my life and for humanity on earth.

When I pray for you I "hear" a victory song. I believe in you because I believe in the power of God's Word in you as you put His Word into action.

Love from Anita Carman

REFLECTION VERSE
[Psalm 90:12] Teach us to number our days aright, that we may gain a heart of wisdom.

REFLECTION QUESTION
What consumes your time that has no eternal value? What must you change to intentionally live a life God rewards?

_____

_____

_____

_____

_____

_____

_____

_____

Day 27

We've always known we're not omnipresent and we can't be at three places at the same time though we keep trying. Don't be surprised when the need for your presence at multiple places at the same time will be accentuated exponentially when you're dealing with the aftermath of a storm. Someone used the word *priority* as if one word will change how multiple needs have been compressed into the same number of hours in a day. But *priority* is not a fix-all word. The fact is, when you wear many hats, multiple areas are priority.

The question then is not who has priority but rather who gets priority the next ten minutes. Life becomes a continuous juggling act of shifting from one need to another and keeping all the spinning plates in the air. When you are operating in this state always remember that a crisis time is a temporary season. Over time, things will get better. Either that, or you'll learn to function in a constant state of crisis and crisis will become your new normal. Meanwhile, don't expect a formula created from human reasoning to solve your problem.

The rule God first, family second, business third, and everyone else fourth doesn't always work because life cannot be fit into a neat package. Sometimes putting God first means focusing on your family or your business or those in need. Instead of trusting a rule, learn to live trusting the voice of the Holy Spirit. Ask God to expand your time, pray for favor, keep the peace when you can, let the small things go, and push life along the best you can. Have the freedom to ask, "Does this have to be done now?" or "Does it have to be done my way as long as it gets done?" Remember God created the night for a reason so try to get your sleep. Problems fall into perspective when we're rested.

When I pray for you I "hear" a victory song. I believe in you because I believe in the power of God's Word in you as you put His Word into action.

Love from Anita Carman

REFLECTION VERSE
[1 Thessalonians 5:16-17] Be joyful always; pray continually...

REFLECTION QUESTION
How have you been running in your own ideas instead of leaning on God's continual wisdom? The key word is "continual". When we develop the need to ask continually, we also keep in continual relationship with God. How has your need for wisdom brought you closer to God?

Day 28

I praise God for the support of those who respond to a need and come to the rescue. What I am learning in the role of the one being rescued is that in order to accept help, you must let go of control. Take, for example, the plumber who came and accidentally opened the gate where I had contained the dogs. When once I could shut a gate, and know it would remain shut, the more people I let into my space, the more I am unable to control how their actions can undo mine. Take another example of how I was so delighted to have retrieved some important papers from the flood and had set them aside where I could find them, only to find that someone walked away with them and packed them in a box without a label. What God is teaching me is that people bring with them their different good intentions and it takes not needing to control every detail so we can fully use the help around us.

At the same time, the model is not to let everyone jump in without a plan. In saving the world, God the Father, God the Son and God the Holy Spirit acted in unison. The divine design is one of community with each member of the Trinity exercising a specific role: God the Father willed it, God the Spirit empowered it, and God the Son did it. And so it is in any project where a community is involved. We must first settle what we are doing before anyone starts working. Then we must define each person's role so we don't step all over each other. The end goal is not to control each other but to be in agreement in a common mission and respect each other's role to accomplish something together. Working together doesn't just happen. It takes following the divine design.

When I pray for you, I "hear" a victory song. I believe in you because I believe in the power of God's Word in you as you put His Word into action.

Love from Anita Carman

REFLECTION VERSE

[2 Chronicles 30:12] Also in Judah the hand of God was on the people to give them unity of mind to carry out what the king and his officials had ordered, following the word of the Lord.

REFLECTION QUESTION

When God led the people to build something, He gave them a plan. God operates with order and design. In rebuilding after a storm, how can you press the pause button and agree on a plan before rushing in to solve a problem? Who should you invite to have a voice in the overall plan?

Day 29

When I got word that the executive pastor of my church was flooded out I immediately asked if he and his wife needed a place to stay. He responded that the church had already found him a safe place to land. Though I did not get to be the one to bless him I was blessed to have offered. In the midst of all the sad stories of losses we get to write a different story.

Our story is about authentic relationships. It's about the electrician who gave us priority because over the years we've grown to become more than just a customer. It's about a volunteer at Inspire Women reaching out to help the staff of the ministry because she saw a financial need and asked her husband to give a donation as his birthday gift to her. It's about my husband and I moving out of our downstairs master bedroom to offer to my son and daughter-in-law the bedroom on the first floor in case my daughter-in-law has a C-section and can't make it up a flight of stairs. It's about taking the word "imposition" or "inconvenience" out of our vocabulary and living in the world of reinventing ourselves and our environment out of love for each other. It's about having the courage to keep leading out of love for the women in our city and to keep building the mission God gave us before the hurricane hit.

The most important lesson was not how to escape from the hurricane (though that is a valuable lesson), the more important lesson was how to keep living and loving in spite of the hurricane. We at Inspire Women are grateful that God allowed the hurricane to impact us as well. We get to lead and to love in the midst of experiencing losses that those we are reaching are experiencing. We don't get to lead from a cocoon but from the midst of a wave that knocked us off our feet.

The Apostle Paul served in the mission God gave him even when life hit him hard. Rocks hit his head and he fell to the ground and was left as dead. But praise God he got up the next day and stayed on mission. Jesus checked on the welfare of his mother and the disciple

John while he was nailed to a cross. He couldn't help with his hands but he helped with whatever part of his body he could use, so he used his mouth and offered words of comfort and direction. We draw from the strength of our relationship with God, with the staff, with volunteers and with our supporters to keep our programs going at full steam to encourage the women who serve in our city. We get to keep going while holding on to each other's hands, and checking on each other. "Are you ok?" we ask. "Then get up, get going, and let's keep changing lives for Jesus!"

When I pray for you I "hear" a victory song. I believe in you because I believe in the power of God's Word in you as you put His Word into action.

Love from Anita Carman

REFLECTION VERSE
[John 17:23] I in them and you in me. May they be brought to complete unity to let the world know that you sent me and have loved them even as you have loved me.

REFLECTION QUESTION
God speaks of a unity in His people that comes from each person submitting their lives under the authority of God's overall mission. It's impossible to have unity when each person is serving his own kingdom. How can you bring unity in your family or community by agreeing to the same shared values and mission? Instead of fighting for one's own interest, how can individuals fight together for the benefit of the whole?

_____

_____

_____

Day 30

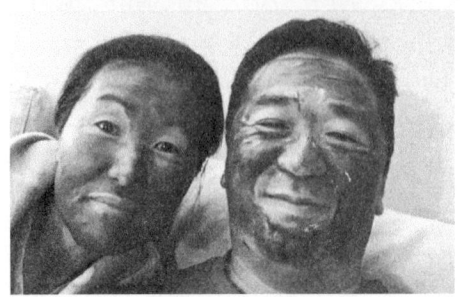

This is not exactly the image you'd expect to see when a couple discovers they didn't escape Hurricane Harvey after all. A beauty mask seems out of place or is it? A couple's facial was how Mia Yoo, the vice president of Inspire Women, and her husband chose to respond. After spending the week rescuing everyone else impacted by the flood, Mia and Joe returned home to discover that water had seeped under their hardwood floors and soaked into the insulation in their sheetrock. As a result, they were staring at a restoration project, expected to last for months. When my husband and I went over in the middle of the night to drop off a dehumidifier, they had just put their two kids to bed.

Before the night was over, they kept to their original schedule to engage in activities to build their marriage. One of those activities included enjoying a facial together.

To me, the image of the mud pack on their faces was a statement that when there's nothing else you can do to change events around you, the next best thing you can do is to invest in each other. Thank God for the person you have beside you in the midst of a storm.

The ages of Mia's children are similar to my sons who were six and eight when our home flooded many years ago. Our family decided the most important thing was to stay safe and to be together. I know Mia and her family will experience as I did with my own children that we don't need things around us to be perfect. What defines us is not the rubble, but we, the family, will rise from the rubble to keep loving and to keep living in spite of the mess. We, the family, choose to seek God's purpose first and to show the world that our love for God and for each other can get us through any storm.

When I pray for you I "hear" a victory song. I believe in you because I believe in the power of God's Word in you as you put His Word into action.

Love from Anita Carman

REFLECTION VERSE

[Deuteronomy 12:7] There, in the presence of the Lord your God, you and your families shall eat and shall rejoice in everything you have put your hand to, because the Lord your God has blessed you.

REFLECTION QUESTION

God's end destination for us is not the pit. Write down your praises while in a valley and say how you will help your family and those around you firm up your relationship with God as you trust His ultimate destination for you is on the mountaintop.

Loss is loss and everyone's loss is personal and painful. My heart goes out to the thousands who may still be in shelters. At the same time my heart also goes out to the thousands who have found refuge in the home of a family member or friend or have leased a new temporary place but are going through the frustration of being far from the children's schools or experiencing the aggravation of not being able to find a matching shoe. You may be thinking, "Stop stressing over a shoe when others have lost a foot."

I must admit this idea of feeling better by comparing ourselves to others who have it worse is a guilt strategy I could never sustain. It forced me into expressing the right behavior on the outside while complaining on the inside. I think the guilt strategy is ineffective for me personally because it reminds me of my childhood formative years when my mother guilted me into eating my carrots because the children in a distant part of the world are starving. It actually made me not want to eat at all! Lately I have found a coping strategy that I believe aligns with God's design.

God does not guilt us into wholeness. He loves us into wholeness. It came to my attention that I have operated with a model where human made perfection became the standard. So, for instance, if I remodeled a house and 99% was done perfectly I will complain and fixate on that one thing that wasn't done quite right. In a time of crisis this perfectionist model can drive us insane. So, the thought hit me, "Why not flip the model?" The Apostle Paul was content in plenty or in want because he began with zero.

When we begin in that place of being nothing and having nothing worth anything but for Christ, then everything we have is an addition. Taking this "Begin with zero" mentality I found myself rejoicing every time I found an item. It was like having Christmas all day long. No longer did I live in the world of "Where's my sock?" as if the world owed me a perfect space with every item in place but I transitioned into the world of "Oh cool!!! I'm no longer at zero! My points are adding up. Here's another sock!" Some people say it's having the right attitude, I see it more as having the right theology. The truth is, we are nothing without Christ, but we have everything in Him and through Him. Every good thing we have comes from God. So, begin with nothing and start adding up and praising God for the reminder that every good thing comes from our Heavenly Father who chooses to show us His grace and provision!

When I pray for you I "hear" a victory song. I believe in you because I believe in the power of God's Word in you as you put His Word into action.

Love from Anita Carman

REFLECTION VERSE
[Philemon 3:8-9] What is more, I consider everything a loss compared to the surpassing greatness of knowing Christ Jesus my Lord, for whose sake I have lost all things. I consider them rubbish, that I may gain Christ.

REFLECTION QUESTION
Do you feel life owes you for all your hard work? Do you feel God owes you for your years of faithfulness? But what if you followed the Apostle Paul and viewed your life as rubbish compared to the greatness of knowing Christ. How does viewing Christ as your greatest treasure change how you view everything else in your life?

Day 32

When we are surrounded by images of destroyed homes, we may find ourselves in conflict with the cheerful images on the front covers of magazines featuring model homes or the latest design in kitchens. We may even berate ourselves for gravitating towards photos of the latest quartz counters or the new pewter color in paints. Is it wrong to want beauty?

The scenes of the homes destroyed by Hurricane Harvey reminded me of the run-down homes with dirt yards I saw on a mission trip in a third world country I visited some years ago. When I returned to U.S. soil from that mission trip, the America I saw around me appeared outrageously prosperous. I found myself disconnecting emotionally from those with perfect homes and manicured lawns. Having order and beauty as a standard felt insensitive and shallow. God had to teach me what the Apostle Paul learned about living in plenty and in want. The idea is to find our joy in God in whatever situation we are in, but that doesn't mean we should feel guilty for appreciating order and beauty.

As part of restoring a flooded home I had the opportunity to visit a design flooring store. At first, I felt bad for being impressed by the beautiful items around me, but at the same time I was surprised by how much the beauty around me lifted my spirit. Then it hit me that beauty is what God designed when He created the world. We reflect God best when we model after Him and accept beauty as the divine standard. Instead of giving up beauty to lower everyone to the same devastated state, why not empower everyone to subdue the earth with God's standards?

If images of destruction are depressing you, try visiting a beautiful showroom, run your hands across the smoothness of a natural marble top, or inspire your imagination to bring order and beauty into your space. Even on a tight budget we can introduce order to our home and put touches of beauty around us. Try bringing in a pretty pot or picture. I made a sign that read, "This is my happy space." I put it on a table near the front door. Just seeing a happy sign made me happy. So, the next time your eyes turn towards beauty, celebrate the divine in you and ask God for His strength to subdue an imperfect world with His standards.

When I pray for you I "hear" a victory song. I believe in you because I believe in the power of God's Word in you as you put His Word into action.

Love from Anita Carman

REFLECTION VERSE
[Genesis 1:31] God saw all that he had made, and it was very good.

REFLECTION QUESTION
How can you introduce beauty back into your life and into your surroundings? How can you draw from knowing that beauty is God's standard to rise above the rubble and build again?

_____

_____

_____

_____

Thank you, Amie ,for showing up with Paul and helping us pack and move! We all need a little help from our friends during the rough seasons in our lives. When you are a giver you may not know what it feels like to receive. You may even find yourself in that awkward place of not knowing how to ask for help. What I have experienced in my times of need is the sweet gift from those who gave when I didn't get the chance to build up my courage to ask. They have been the first responders in my life. They anticipated the need even before I was personally aware of the need. Givers usually are disconnected from their own needs because they are so busy taking care of everyone else. These first responders strengthened me and I, in turn, was empowered to bless those around me so they could be encouraged to keep serving.

When I look back at what kept my spirit from sinking into the pit, I realize it was a lot of little things. It was the individuals who showed up to help me pack. It was the person who lent me his truck to move. It was the neighbor who brought a meal. It was the leader who secured an auction item for our ministry's luncheon. It was the trainer who took the dogs to help them understand the new pecking order with a new baby in the house. It was the friend who let me control the agenda because I needed to feel there was still something in life within my control. It was the person I could ask to cancel everything and just sit beside me, because in the midst of all the changes, I just needed to see one unchanging person I could be sure of. The fact is, we don't get through with just one helping hand, we need a little help from many places. In a crisis, God shows us the power of community. When each person responds according to what each can do, we get through the storm together.

When I pray for you, I "hear" a victory song. I believe in you because I believe in the power of God's Word in you as you put His Word into action.

Love from Anita Carman

REFLECTION VERSE
[2 Corinthians 1:3-4] Praise be to the God and Father of our Lord Jesus Christ, the Father of compassion and the God of all comfort, who comforts us in all our troubles, so that we can comfort those in any trouble with the comfort we ourselves receive from God.

REFLECTION QUESTION
What comfort do you need from God so you, in turn, can offer comfort to others? What if God chose to give you comfort through those around you? What humility must you express to ask for and to receive help?

God's Word reminds us that this earth will one day pass away. The admonition is to hold loosely to our worldly possessions and to focus on building what has eternal consequences. At the same time God's Word also tells us that faith without works is dead. So, while doing good works to restore houses destroyed by a hurricane, how do we reconcile God's admonition to build what's eternal? I believe the answer is to remember that when we restore a house, the effort is not to save a building but to restore a home.

Restoring a home means restoring stability to a family. It means putting the children back in their neighborhood and in school. It means the conversations around the dinner table can be redirected to our relationships and not our things. It means when we bring stability back into our lives we can dream again and not be in a state of limbo, waiting for things to be repaired. However, while restoring the physical infrastructure that supports stability, God expects those with eyes of faith to protect what has eternal consequences. This means recognizing that whereas non-believers will give to a hurricane relief fund for the physical welfare of the community, believers are the only ones who will give to missions and ministry and protect the eternal souls of humanity.

Amid additional expenses, we need to look at our rainy day fund the way Joseph tapped into his store house in the midst of a famine. The executive pastor of my church said, "We save for a rainy day so here's a rainy day. Use your rainy day fund!" His words freed me to use my rainy day fund to stabilize my family and God's ministries! For all the times I taught my children to save, here's my chance to show them how much better life is when you saved for a rainy day. If you have a rainy day fund, don't live in a world of unnecessary angst from the pressure of unexpected financial needs. Instead, break that piggy bank jar and thank God for the gift of preparation and spread the relief.

When I pray for you, I "hear" a victory song. I believe in you because I believe in the power of God's Word in you as you put His Word into action.

Love from Anita Carman

REFLECTION VERSE

[Genesis 41:56-57] When the famine had spread over the whole country, Joseph opened the storehouses and sold grain to the Egyptians, for the famine was severe throughout Egypt. And all the countries came to Egypt to buy grain from Joseph, because the famine was severe in all the world.

REFLECTION QUESTION

What reserve have you prepared that can be used for your family, your church, the ministries you support and for your community? Like Joseph, who opened the storehouse to reach those beyond Pharaoh's household, what is God calling you to do beyond your own family?

_____

_____

_____

_____

_____

_____

_____

I am reliving a chunk of my son's life that I missed when he left home to go out of state for college. He left the nest at 18 years old, and eleven years later he still finds his parent's home his safe landing place after a storm. This time he brings his wife and baby boy. In our time together, I observed that much has changed and yet not that much has changed. I remember him as that teenager who always beat the next video game, which meant he was often immersed in a video game.

These days I still find him engrossed in a video but this time it was a video on what to pack to bring to the hospital when it was time for the baby's delivery. He was watching a video featuring a doctor explaining what it meant to induce labor. Or reading a book about becoming a new father. When did the boy's interests evolve into the interest of the man in his household? I felt as if I was given back a chunk of time and was living in slow motion the transition of my little boy into the man who researches every detail to care for his wife and new family.

I used to jump on him for being consumed with his video games, missing the fact that he beat the game every time. From a young age he learned victory in a simulation of life through his games, where he battled and overcame unexpected foes. And now I see him watching videos on life experiences to prepare for any deviation ahead of him in the birth of his first-born. In our chats I am rewriting history. I never knew his brother, who drove him to school in high school, found humor in making him late to the point of 29 tardies that almost caused him to lose credit for the class. I never knew because he never accused his brother. They were and continue to be as tight as can be, even when they are on different paths. While he's preparing to be a dad, his brother is out of the country serving as an attorney on site in Japan.

As I pondered the gaps in life, my son was filling them in like an anchorman in Eyewitness News. I was reminded the Bible tells me that God who watches over us never slumbers. In my absence God was omnipresent. In my half knowledge God was all knowing. In my imperfection God remained perfect. My trust is in the God who embraced the sons I raised and took the boys on their own journeys to become men. The umbilical cord was cut long ago. The fact is, today my sons don't really need me to be here for them to make it. But I get to be here to watch God grow and lead them. And that's when life is most beautiful. It's when we are in each other's lives not because we are needy but because we are blessed.

When I pray for you I "hear" a victory song. I believe in you because I believe in the power of God's Word in you as you put His Word into action.

Love from Anita Carman

REFLECTION VERSE
[2 Timothy 1:6] ...I remind you to fan into flame the gift of God, which is in you through the laying on of my hands.

REFLECTION QUESTION
Don't waste insights you learned in your yesteryears. What lessons did you learn in your formative years that will help you get through the challenges you face today?

_____

_____

_____

_____

_____

The day before Baby Ezra, my first grandson, was expected to arrive, I had butterflies in my stomach thinking about the safety of the baby, the labor pains of the mother, the fact that my son was becoming a father, and the emotional state of their dog who may realize for the first time in her life that she's a pup and not the first born. In the aftermath of Hurricane Harvey, we settled the chaos caused by the flood as best we could and as fast as we could so we could get on to the business of life. What a great incentive to get life organized so we can welcome more life and new dreams and new beginnings!

I am excited about experiencing more love and being reminded yet again that life is all about the ones we love. It's about sharing life with one another. It's about watching how love does not diminish when you share it with more people but the energy of all the people around you who are loved by you somehow creates a love cloud. It's hard to explain but those in a love cloud are cushioned by each other through the bumps in life. In the Bible, God's presence was represented through a cloud. In fact, when the cloud moved Moses directed the people to pull up the stakes of their tents and move with the cloud. There is safety when you live under the protection of a love cloud.

When I was uprooted years ago from my country I wandered around for a season looking for a place of belonging. Today, God has taught me that we find our place of belonging when we connect with people who love us. And if we can't find people to love us then that's our cue to create a community where others can be loved by us. So, step into a "love cloud" or create one. Either way, don't live without one!

When I pray for you, I "hear" a victory song. I believe in you because I believe in the power of God's Word in you as you put His Word into action.

Love from Anita Carman

REFLECTION VERSE
[1 Corinthians 13:6-7] Love…always protects, always trusts, always hopes, always perseveres.

REFLECTION QUESTION
How can you lean on love to build a safe community? How can love protect the interests of all parties and compel you to persevere with each other even when the odds are against you?

My grandson was born on September 14, 2017. My first impression of Ezra Townsend Carman was not his eye color or hair (though he had a lot of it.) What caught my attention was how big he was. He arrived during the aftermath of Hurricane Harvey and he looked ready to take on the world. Since my son and daughter-in-law moved in with me after the flood, Ezra will start out life in Grammy's home. I started to think about the important things I wanted Ezra to know.

I wanted him to know that it's not important if he looks like his dad or his grandfather or any other member in the family. He was not born to reflect the image of a family member but to reflect God's image. I wanted him to know that although I look forward to him being a big and strong man the same way he is a big and strong baby, he won't have the pressure of feeling he must save his family because we already have a Savior in Jesus. I wanted him to know Grammy just wants him to be everything God designed him to be when God wove him in his mother's womb. I wanted him to know he has a safe place in our hearts, where he is loved unconditionally as he is on this very first day of his existence when he hasn't done one thing but breathe. I wanted him to know there will be hurricanes in life but with preparation and courage, we can rise above the tidal waves that sometimes knock us off our feet. There were so many things I wanted to share with Ezra as I held him and I asked God for the gift of time to do so.

I have heard people say that there is nothing like holding your first grandchild and now I know why. I get to do for my grandchildren what I did for my children while adjusting the parts I wanted to do better. I get to feel again those feelings I felt when I held my sons in my arms: I felt love more than I ever dreamed possible, I felt a new optimism no matter how the odds were against us, I felt a deep trust in God who birthed the next generation as evidence that He is not through with accomplishing His purpose on earth and He will still use us to do it. So, Ezra, my first grandson, welcome to planet earth. I salute you as a leader in the making and a future warrior for an eternal kingdom.

Love from Anita Carman,

Ezra's Grammy
and the Founder and President of Inspire Women

REFLECTION VERSE
[Psalm 100:5] For the Lord is good and his love endures forever; his faithfulness continues through all generations.

REFLECTION QUESTION
How will you teach God's faithfulness and goodness to the next generation? What miracles or spiritual lessons have you experienced that you wish to document for the exhortation of generations to come?

Day 38

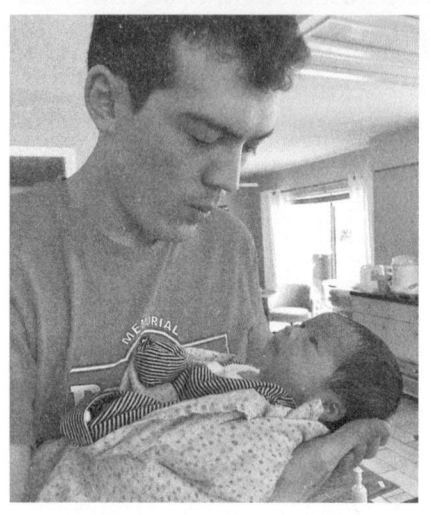

Words cannot express the emotion I feel in my heart at that special moment caught on camera of my son looking into the face of his new-born. The picture of my son delighting in his son is such a reminder to me of how God our heavenly Father delights in us. The Bible tells me that we are "the apple of [His] eye." God our Father wove us in our mother's womb and ordained each day of our lives.

In the aftermath of a physical hurricane or a personal hurricane in our lives, we all need a picture that reminds us how much we are loved. The picture of my son looking into the face of his son inspires me to imagine another picture—that of my heavenly Father looking into my face and wanting me to see what He sees in me and what He sees for me. In the same way it would break my son's heart if Ezra who is so loved does not grow up to claim everything his father wants for him, God our heavenly Father does not want us to settle for debris and devastation when His love for us will empower us to take our place on the mountaintop of life. The devil will attempt to get us to accuse God or to doubt God's love for us. He knows that for someone so loved as we are, we are unstoppable.

When I pray for you, I "hear" a victory song. I believe in you because I believe in the power of God's Word in you as you put His Word into action.

Love from Anita Carman

REFLECTION VERSE

[Psalm 17:8-9] Keep me as the apple of your eye; hide me in the shadow of your wings from the wicked who assail me, from my mortal enemies who surround me.

REFLECTION QUESTION

How does knowing you are the apple of God's eye influence how you think about yourself and the life God wants you to have? What must you give up in order to receive God's best for you?

Perhaps you see yourself as being able to juggle multiple balls in the air. I've always enjoyed multi-processing. However, over the years, God had to teach me to handle multiple areas while keeping my focus on relationship and not just the task. For example, Moses was called to reach the Promise Land with the people but if he made it only about getting to the destination he might defeat God's purpose and end up getting to the Promise Land all by himself, without the people! In any divine appointment always remember, we are called to reach the destination with the people because God is all about people. Be careful not to focus on the task and forget the people!

The end goal is love and relationship, which explains the image you see with me with a cell phone on one hand and my four-day old grand baby in the other. I was dressed to go to work but needed to be in the house because the plumber was coming. My son and daughter-in-law who moved in with me after their house flooded were exhausted from being up with the baby all night. I was happy to hold Ezra while they took a break to make themselves a creamed bagel.

I remember those days when my son was a baby and felt like a permanent appendage. Sitting down to have a bagel felt like such a luxury! As I held Ezra so he felt secure and stopped crying I wanted him to hear his Grammy ministering words of hope to others who survived the storm. He is learning from a young age that we are called to love each other in the family but we were not sent by God to love only our own family. My friend Jill Briscoe used to say, "You have more than one family!" Ezra might as well learn this lesson of loving multiple families at a young age. As he goes in and out of his sleep cycles he will hear his family loving others. The Apostle Paul said in the Bible that we are to imitate him. The next generation won't know what love looks like unless we live it out in front of them. I pray Ezra will grow up to know no other way but to love those around him. I pray that loving will be his normal.

When I pray for you I "hear" a victory song. I believe in you because I believe in the power of God's Word in you as you put His Word into action.

Love from Anita Carman

REFLECTION VERSE
[1 Timothy 1:5] The goal of this command is love, which comes from a pure heart and a good conscience and a sincere faith.

REFLECTION QUESTION
How has your life turned into being more about the project than the people the project helps? How can you rearrange activities so the people you are helping will feel loved along the way, while you're finishing a project that benefits them?

_____

_____

_____

_____

_____

_____

Day 40

Before I pat myself on the back and view myself as Wonder Woman for helping others, I need to stop in my tracks and give credit where credit is due. I know that any joy in my service comes from an emotional reservoir that is full. But how does an emotional reservoir get full? I know that my emotional reservoir is full because as soon as my world is sent into a tailspin, I am surrounded by family and sisters-in-Christ who show up in my life. They give me the gift of their presence, their organization skills, and their resolve to get me back on my feet as soon as possible. I am only able to minister to others because someone loved me enough to minister to me.

I think the fallacy is to think that ministry leaders are above pain, can fend for themselves and exist to give and give and to give some more. I am saddened when ministry leaders feel that their only value is when they are able to give. When we operate out of performance it is a sure recipe towards burnout and resentment. What God wants is for the shepherd to love the sheep but also for the sheep to love the shepherd. Let me get up again, girded by God's love and the love of His faithful saints. Let me serve again, out of worshipping a worthy God whose good continues in spite of the storm. Let me give again because (praise God) someone took the time to give to me! Let me serve from a place of gratitude and a heart that cries out, "I love because God first loved me. I serve because someone first poured into my life. Thank you God and thank you to all the kind souls who took the time to love me!"

When I pray for you, I "hear" a victory song. I believe in you because I believe in the power of God's Word in you as you put His Word into action.

Love from Anita Carman

REFLECTION VERSE:
[1 John 4:19-20] We love because he first loved us.

REFLECTION QUESTION
Who are the individuals who have invested in your life? When was the last time you wrote them a thank you note or called to check on them? Is today the day you will take the time to thank God for loving you first and for all the kind souls who poured into your life?

Losses have a way of stirring up other losses. You may find yourself grieving again and not know why. Let yourself grieve. Don't stuff it away. Then, you can get on with God's new plans for you. The grief may be from your battle with your flesh and with your spirit. God's spirit wants to birth something new, but your flesh holds on to what you want. We fight for dreams that don't even make us happy. But, it's our dream and we want it. "This is my life!" we say, but God says, "No." We don't own anything, not even your life. Every breath we take is a grace gift. Begin there and realize that we have nothing. And, now we're an empty canvas on which God can paint the picture for our lives.

The hurricane paused everything because there are bottlenecks with everything. Bottlenecks happen because wounded people go slower, overworked contractors go slower, insurance adjusters go slower. With the forced GO SLOW! signs everywhere, now there's time to reflect, time for flashbacks.

Let me share with you the flashbacks I've been having that led to some healthy wholesome conversation with God, with myself and with those around me. Here are four lessons I learned.

LESSON 1: The paths we give up open up new paths

In holding my grandbaby, I was reminded of how frustrated I felt when I left corporate America for my baby. The fact was, I wanted the path in corporate America. I wanted to be partner. But, God had other plans. I had no family in Houston. There was no mother or mother-in-law or aunt I could ask to help watch my baby. When my son had asthma, I was afraid to leave him in a nursery. What if someone didn't catch that he was having trouble breathing? So, I laid down my career for my baby. I don't expect him to understand and I don't bring it up. I don't say to him, "You owe me, look what I gave up for you!" Instead, I believed, for reasons I did not understand at the time, that God wanted me home. From the loss emerged a new path. Because I was home, I went to seminary. I didn't know where God was going, but my choice was to follow. You must give up your dreams before you can receive God's new dream for you. If you need to die every day to your self, you didn't die enough the first time. Stop taking yourself off the altar. You'll get to God's dream faster if you die to self and stay dead. Then, you're ready for the resurrection. Until then, you'll still be on the cross. It takes being dead before God can move on to the resurrection.

LESSON 2: Raise the boy and give her the man

My son and daughter-in-law moved in after the flood. I've heard people say you can't have two women in the same house. I've heard people say a mother-in-law and a daughter-in-law never get along. Since I thought my daughter-in-law and I had a great relationship, I was curious how that happened. My ponderings led me into a conversation with my son and daughter-in-law with their new son in our midst. I told them I figured out why people say what they say about the mother-in-law and the daughter-in-law. So, I said to Daphne, "You, now, have a little boy like I did. While holding the baby it reminded me of my days with my little boy. I remembered, when he was in preschool, he was so excited for me to visit on

Mother's Day. He was part of a mini-production at school. He made me a painting. I still have it. And he sang to me. I still remember the words: "You are my sunshine my only sunshine. You make me happy when skies are grey. You'll never know mom how much I love you. Please don't take my sunshine away (Davis, Mitchell, 1939)." Daphne, I want you to know the Bible says a man must leave his mother and father, and he and the woman he marries will be one. I used to be the most important woman in my son's life, but I no longer have that position. You, now, are the most important woman in his life, as it should be, as God ordained it to be. I trust in God's design. So, this is what I get to do as your mother-in-law. I got to raise the boy and give you the man.

Dr. Henry Cloud said in one of his books that when a child leaves, you will feel it in your heart like a ripping of your flesh. Your job as mother is to feel the rip and let go anyway (Cloud, Townsend, 2015).

People talk about love a lot and romanticize it but to truly love is a painful thing. It was painful for Jesus and we shouldn't be surprised if it's painful for us.

LESSON 3: Life is about the people we loved along the way

This lesson came from a fashback of the memorial service of the wife of the retired pastor of Houston's First Baptist Church, which took place shortly after Hurricane Harvey.

I went to the service of Uldine Bisagno, the wife of Brother John Bisagno. I remember the time she needed a place to store her furniture and I offered my house. She gave me two antique chairs that are at Inspire Women headquarters and a page from an old museum-quality bible, which she said was worth a lot of money. She was the one who instructed me to take time to decorate my house and show that I paid attention to details in the home. She said that every space should be intentional, "Use each shelf, each corner well. Don't just scatter stuff everywhere." Knowing how well she managed her home, her son's testimony at her service touched me. He said she was home with in-home hospice care. She watched as water filled her home. They had to evacuate her in a wheelchair to take her to an off-site hospice. On the way out, she was not upset her house flooded. She said, "I'm going to live with Jesus." She passed shortly afterwards. They closed the service with a video of Pastor Bisagno and Uldine, when they were younger, singing on stage the song, Side by Side. Then, the camera went directly to a shot of Pastor Bisagno in his eighties and in a wheelchair. With the casket in front of him, he started to sing the same song as robustly as he could. The words were written by Harry M. Woods in 1927:

> *Oh, we ain't got a barrel of money*
> *Maybe we're ragged and funny*
> *But we travel along, singin' our song*
> *Side by side.*

> *Don't know what's comin' tomorrow*
> *Maybe it's trouble and sorrow*
> *But we travel the road, sharin' our load*
> *Side by side.*

Seeing my pastor in his wheelchair sing the song alone while his wife laid in a casket in front of him, my mind was reminded of all the special relationships in my life. At the end of the day, life is never about the things we have. It's about the people we loved and the people who loved us along the way. God did not die for stuff. He died for people. If we forget that life is about people, then we will have lived in vain.

LESSON 4: Find the good in every setback

This lesson came from a flashback of the memorial service of Jo Beth Young, the wife of Dr. Ed Young, which also happened shortly after Hurricane Harvey.

The son of Dr. Ed Young and Jo Beth Young shared a time when he was a young preacher. His dad invited him to say the prayer at the 11 a.m. service. It was the most attended service and it was televised. He wrote his prayer down, memorized it, and even laminated it. His cue to get on stage was a nod from the choir director. He got his nod and he was on. His voice filled the room. His prayer went beautifully. Then, he ended with the Our Father and invited the audience to say it with him. He said, "Our Father." They repeated, "Our Father." He said, "Hallowed be thy name." They said, "Hallowed be thy name." And, then, he choked. He could not remember the next line. He said the audience tried to help him by feeding him the next line, but it was a disaster. He finally just ended the prayer abruptly by saying something like, "For thine is the power and the glory forever, Amen," and went and sat down. The seat he was in happened to be right next to his mother. He was feeling totally defeated and embarrassed when she leaned over and whispered in his ears and said, "Your voice sounded so great up there."

His point was, she was an encourager all her life. He saw it as his having blown it. She saw it as he proved he had a great preacher's voice.

We can find good in every setback. It's just where you choose to look. My house did not flood this time, but served as refuge for my son whose house flooded. Years ago, my house did flood. I thought it was the worse day of my life. But, today, I saw how my son was not rattled by the storm. The reason is because we have been through a flood together. He's a veteran now. God used a temporary flood event in my son's formative years to teach him how to get through a storm.

So, here's the good I see in the flood God allowed in my life years ago during my son's formative years. Today, I get to see that God has prepared my son. I am given the gift of seeing that my son is ready to take on the storms in his life. And isn't that what we long to see in our children? We want to know they have what it takes in them to keep going no matter what storm they face.

Don't let a temporary problem derail you. Find the good in it and stay on course and on track with God's mission.

When my son and daughter-in-law moved in, they brought their two dogs. With my own two dogs, we now had four dogs in the house. Shortly after the baby was born on September 14th and came home, I noticed the four dogs acted like a pack and they all charged over to the baby. I was nervous they might think the baby was a squirrel and start pouncing on him. So, I brought them to a dog expert who explained to me the psychology of how a dog thinks. He said there are no equals. You don't even have a president and vice president. What you have in the canine world is one leader who is top dog and every other dog in the pack follows. He said Ebony, my 70-pound labradoodle, follows Ivory, the golden retriever. "How do you know that?" I asked. He said, "Look how Ebony always looks at Ivory. Not once does Ivory ever look at Ebony." He said the leader does not take direction from a subordinate. Then, he assessed my son and daughter-in-law's dogs. He said Chibi, the miniature labradoodle, is the leader because she doesn't listen to anyone. She thinks they are all her subordinates. Kobe, the American Eskimo, listens and sub-mits to authority. He said Chibi is also anxious because she thinks she's the leader while she doesn't have the ability to lead. So, that's the reason why she's nervous. If she can settle down to her role as follower, she will be fine. His input made me think about my own life. There are days I'm like Chibi. I think God is my subordinate and I don't listen to Him. I usurp his position and take the lead and I end up a basket case. I do best when I settle into my position as follower and let God lead. God led me out of corporate America into a new path. He led me to let go of my son and give him to my daughter-in-law. He led me to hold lightly to temporary things and focus on the eternal. He led me to find good in every setback and to stay on course and on mission.

I pray that in your flashbacks you will find clarity as well for your life. Now, let's look at the reflection questions and find clarity from flashbacks in your life

REFLECTION QUESTION 1: What event did you witness from a loss or a physical personal tsunami in your life that caused you to say, "One day I will...?" What did you want to change? Did you want to build a different life, a different world? How can you use flashbacks to clarify your purpose or the pattern with which you are to pursue your purpose?

_____

_____

_____

_____

_____

REFLECTION QUESTION 2: In a crisis, things move quickly. Did someone not help you like you wanted him or her to? What flashbacks hurt your heart? If, instead of focusing on flashbacks that wound you, what can you focus on that reminds you of God's deliverance and blessings?

_____

_____

_____

_____

_____

REFLECTION QUESTION 3: When life is chaotic, there is always someone who missed a cue. Did someone do or say the wrong thing at the wrong time? Do you have a negative flashback of a conversation or incident that keeps resurfacing and upsetting you? What does Jesus' declaration "It is finished" mean to you in relation to your flashbacks or a current situation in your life? Is there someone you need to forgive so you can move forward without dragging a grudge with you the rest of your life?

References

Anderson, Hans Christian, 1846 (public domain). The Princess and the Pea, Denmark: C.A. Reitzel.

Cloud, Henry and Townsend, John, 2015. *Our Mothers, Ourselves: How Understanding Your Mother's Influence Can Set You On A Path To A Better Life*, USA: Zondervan.

Davis, Jimmie and Mitchell, Charles, 1939. *You are My Sunshine*, USA: Peer Music.

Wood, Harry M., 1927. *Side by Side*, Shapiro Bernstein & Co. Inc.

Notes

_____

_____

_____

_____

_____

_____

_____

_____